First Fruits

Other books by the Author:

Shadows from the Rising Sun

Christian Stewardship and Church Finance

Giving is Overflowing

First Fruits

Stewardship Thoughts and Stories from Around the World

Paul R. Lindholm

Hope Publishing House
Pasadena, California

Copyright © 1993 Paul R. Lindholm

All rights reserved.

For information address:
Hope Publishing House
Southern California Ecumenical Council
P. O. Box 60008
Pasadena, California 91116 - U.S.A.
Telephone (818) 792-6123; FAX (818) 792-2121

Cover design - Michael McClary/The Workshop

Printed in the U.S.A. on acid-free paper.

Library of Congress Cataloging-in-Publication Data

Lindholm, Paul R., 1903-
    First fruits : stewardship thoughts and stories from around the world / Paul R. Lindholm.
      p.   cm.
    ISBN 0-932727-67-0 : $18.95. -- ISBN 0-932727-66-2 (pbk.) : $11.95
    1. Stewardship, Christian. I. Title
BV772.L488   1993
248'.6--dc20   93-15679
[B]   CIP

Grateful Acknowledgements

are made to:

Eilene Mendez who faithfully typed the manuscript for this volume; to my wife, Clara, for improving the composition of many of its pages; to Alan Hamilton and to the national church leaders in many countries who planned the stewardship seminars and to the participants of the seminars out of which much of the thoughts and many of the stories of this volume grew.   —*Paul R. Lindholm*
Westminster Gardens
Duarte, California

Contents

Introduction — *Alan Hamilton* 13
Prologue 17

Part 1
Basic Principles of Christian Stewardship

1. God is the Supreme Ruler over All 23
2. God's Intent for All 29
3. God is the Creator, Sustainer and Owner of All 33
4. All are God's Stewards 37
5. Stewards are Accountable to God 41
6. Faithful Stewards Serve Out of Gratitude 45
7. The Great Purpose of Christian Stewardship is to Glorify God 49

Part 2
Four Major Stewardship Responsibilities

8. The Highest Stewardship Responsibility is for the Gospel 57
9. Stewardship Responsibility for Time 63
10. Stewardship Responsibility for Talent 67
11. Stewardship Responsibility for Treasure . . . 71

Part 3
The Christian Steward As A Giver

	Introduction 79
12.	General Biblical Instructions 81
	Question 1: Is any person bypassed in the invitation to give? 81
	Question 2: What quality of gifts is suitable? 83
	Question 3: What is a commendable attitude to have in giving? 85
	Question 4: To whom does the Christian give when giving according to the Holy Scriptures? 87
	Question 5: What are some specific opportunities for giving? 88
	Question 6: How is the amount given to be determined? 92
13.	Motives for Giving 95
	Wrong Motives
	• For self-glory 95
	• For personal material gain 97
	• With hope of achieving merit 97
	• To be relieved of pressure 98
	Good Motives
	• To express gratitude 99
	• To express love 101
	• The desire to honor God 104
	• The desire to share in Christ's continuing mission 105

Table of Contents

Part 4
Results for the Faithful and Wise Steward

	Introduction 111
14.	Experience Fullness of Life 113
15.	Opportunity for More Service 115
16.	Encounters Special Joy 117
17.	Will be Honored by God 119
18.	Has an Intimate Relationship with God .. 121
	Epilogue 123

Introduction

It is he [the risen, ascended Christ] who has given some to be apostles, some prophets, some evangelists, some pastors and teachers, to equip God's people for work in his service, for the building up of the body of Christ (Ep 4:11, 12).

The materials gathered in this book provide abundant evidence that Paul Lindholm is a person whom the ascended Christ has given to the Church in more than 50 countries on five continents as a pastor and teacher. There are varieties of gifts, says the apostle Paul in 1 Corinthians 12, and the particular gift of Paul Lindholm is evidently that of inculcating a clear vision of what the Christian community must understand by "stewardship."

Convinced that this concept has often been limited and limiting, Dr. Lindholm has moved among us with an illuminating and invigorating vision of what the Church can be and do when every member is committed to a total stewardship of life.

After the Lindholms' 23 years of missionary service in China and the Philippines, the Presbyterian Church

(USA) set him free to respond to calls that were coming from across the world. Someone at headquarters was assigned simply to facilitate and coördinate his travels. As his experiences accumulated, so did the graphic and printed materials that extended his outreach, most notably the book, *Christian Stewardship and Church Finance,* published in various editions and languages.

As one of those who coördinated Paul Lindholm's schedule, the undersigned was privileged to sense at firsthand the effectiveness of his ministry: seeing him at work in seminars in Latin America, visiting him in India where he served for two years as stewardship secretary of the National Christian Council, and corresponding with the churches that called him back a second and a third time to repeat and enlarge upon his earlier presentations.

Dr. William Wysham, who also coördinated the Lindholm program, when presiding at a meeting in this country at which Paul was to speak, told of the words of a church leader in Africa in the closing session of a seminar:

> Mr. Lindholm, get some rest back home with Mrs. Lindholm, then both of you come again to spend the rest of your lives with us. I promise you that at the end we'll give each of you a first-class funeral.

Now in active retirement, he shares with us in this book a wealth of his experience and his understanding of

Introduction

stewardship. The Church, now faced with so great a task as a new millennium draws near, will do well to listen carefully to this servant whom the ascended Christ has given to us. —*Alan Hamilton*

Former secretary for Stewardship Education Development of the Presbyterian Commission on Ecumenical Mission and Relations; missionary educator in Ecuador, Venezuela and Costa Rica.

Prologue

In the capital of a central American country the Christian Council of the city sponsored a week of long evening sessions for the study of Christian Stewardship.

At the end, the chair of the program said, "I have been a church member 28 years. Why is it that this week has been my first chance to learn about Christian Stewardship?"

I broke the silence that followed by saying that I was confident that he had learned about it from his Bible reading, from Sunday school lessons, from sermons he had heard, but he may not have had in hand stewardship study materials that had enabled him to examine the subject intensively.

He agreed, and then urged that the materials that we had used for the week be reproduced locally and be made available to the churches. Plans for the doing of that were immediately agreed upon and that study material was a forerunner of the contents of this volume.

The study of Christian Stewardship involves more than acquiring additional knowledge. Near the end of a four-day seminar on this subject, a church officer arose and said, "I must leave now in order to be in my office in time in the morning, but, thank God! I'm not leaving the same person that I was when I came."

In the closing session of another seminar one person stood and said, "If churches use this material it will stir up some of them a bit. I must confess that I have been shook up a bit myself."

Because *living* Christian Stewardship has so much to do with the Christian's basic and primary relationship with God, The Master, Part I of this volume especially deals with how the steward is to relate to **THE ONE** who calls us to be stewards.

Part 1

Seven Basic Principles

of Christian Stewardship

1

God is the Supreme Ruler over All

A young woman is reported to have said to a pastor, "I have five minutes before my bus leaves. Please tell me all you know about God."

Yet referring to only one aspect of God's being, a poet penned these lines:

> Could we with ink the ocean fill,
> And were the skies of parchment made;
> Were every stalk on earth a quill,
> And every one a scribe by trade;
> To write the love of God above
> Would drain the ocean dry,
> Nor could the scroll contain the whole
> Though stretched from sky to sky.
> —*F. M. Lehman*

An Old Testament passage that encapsulates this attempt to describe God is that superb prayer of dedication offered by King David after tremendous contributions made by everyone in the land had poured in for the building of the great temple in Jerusalem:

> *Thine, O Lord, is the greatness and the power and the glory and the victory and the majesty, for all that is in the heavens and the earth is thine; thine is the kingdom, O Lord, and thou art exalted as head above all* (1 Ch 29:11).

This was the passage I used as the theme-verse for three seminars which I gave in an African country a few years ago. During my stay, the Christian education director of a large Protestant denomination had been my interpreter.

As I was leaving the country, she said to me, "If I received nothing else from my participation in these seminars, the discovery of that verse of David's dedicatory prayer would have been ample reward."

What the poet Lehman says about the immeasurable love of God can also be said about the greatness, the power, the glory and the victory and the majesty of God. If we try to imagine the circumstances in which David's prayer was made it will be clear that the five descriptive words that the king used for God had a much greater effect on *his* hearers than they have on hearers today.

Because God's greatness is beyond human comprehension, the Bible repeatedly calls us to think of God at times when we are free of distractions:

> *Be still and know that I am God* (Ps 46:10).

The clear implication here is that there is much more to knowing God than mere words can reveal.

The prophet Habakkuk, who made the well-known declaration that *"the righteous shall live by faith"* (2:4) emphasized the importance of the call to silence before God by making the call world-wide:

> *The Lord is in God's holy temple; let all the earth keep silence before God* (2:20).

Unfortunately in our faith community there is little emphasis on the greatness and the majesty of God, just as there is little stress made on knowing and honoring God with all our heart, soul, mind and strength.

This notion was confirmed in another mission seminar where again I had led a study of King David's prayer praising God's greatness, power, glory, victory and majesty. My interpreter, a retired principal of a teachers' training college, said to me afterwards with tears in his eyes, "One thing weighs heavily on my heart; we don't give honor to God as we should."

The great hymnbook of the Bible, the Psalms, which so often stresses the greatness of God, ends with the appropriate extortion:

> *Let everything that breathes praise the Lord!*
> (150:6).

Near the beginning of that last Psalm is the call:

Praise the Lord according to God's exceeding greatness! (150:2).

I often refer those who claim they have found difficulty in thinking of God as a sovereign, supreme ruler, to the helpful words of George A. Buttrick in his *Faith and Education:*

> If the doctor prescribes penicillin for our pneumonia, we would be foolish to refuse [to take it] on the ground that [the doctor's] procedure is not democratic, or if a judge in mercy were to open the prison cell with a command to the prisoner to act like a good citizen, the liberated [person] could hardly claim that the command is coercive (p. 27).

In reflecting on a large international church conference where delegates heard scores of addresses by speakers from many parts of the world, an internationally known religious commentator pointed out that although there had been much emphasis on rescuing souls, little had been said about "the crown rights of the Redeemer."

Yes, our Redeemer is Sovereign as well as Savior.

In the last book of the Bible there are many echoes of those praises of God's greatness and sovereignty such as are found in the Psalms. The writer paints word-pictures of great multitudes from all nations and tribes sounding forth in tremendous volume, praising *"the King of kings, Lord of lords!"*

The great Handel was so inspired by meditating on such scenes that he was moved to produce the glorious composition, *"The Messiah,"* with which choirs throughout the world stir audiences into ecstasy.

One psalmist declared, *"God's greatness is unsearchable."* God transcends time and space. Astronomers repeatedly have to expand their conceptions of outer space.

The local newspaper reported the other day that "a newly discovered sheet of galaxies stretches for 500 light years . . . about six trillion miles." Even scientists find it difficult to comprehend such spaces. Yet God not only conceived it, what's more, God created it and keeps it all in place.

God is transcendent and God's greatness is, in many ways, a mystery. But rather than be troubled by these realities, we should rejoice at them. If God were not, in being and in works, greater than what the most able human mind could possibly comprehend, then God would not be God and, moreover, would not be in a position to rule over all and be worshiped by all.

It is my firm conviction that with Christian stewardship, the most basic principle that should govern our thinking and be the first step towards learning and practicing meaningful stewardship is our understanding of the fact that:

GOD IS THE SUPREME RULER OVER ALL.

The sovereignty of God is not merely a thought-provoking idea. It is a profound reality to be acknowledged and lived by with heart, soul, mind and strength.

How is it possible we could think we know all that is important to know about God? Even Moses at age 120 prayed:

> *O Lord God, thou hast only begun to show thy servant thy greatness* . . . (Dt 3:24).

2

God's Intent for All

The Creator's first instruction to humankind was: *"Be fruitful."* Render service.

The redemptive purpose of God for us, as revealed in the Holy Scriptures, is not simply that we will be forgiven and be able to rejoice in a blessed eternal life, but rather it is the reward of being restored to a loving relationship with God, one in which we will gladly render God faithful service.

To the early believers in Ephesus the apostle Paul stated this principle clearly:

> *For we are God's workmanship, created in Christ Jesus for good works* (Ep 2:10).

To call God "Lord" and yet not be concerned about rendering God service is a mockery to God. It gives no indication of understanding the meaning of the word "lord."

Those who ignore God, who can be numbered with the unredeemed, commonly lay emphasis on life's personal rewards, allotting to themselves the attention and service that in actuality is due God.

This is idolatry. It is harmful to the self and, perhaps for that reason most of all, displeases God. Consider the temptation, faced by all of us, to indulge in self-centered behavior. We can understand why Jesus stressed the need to love and serve God, and then others, with all our heart.

In his autobiography, Sherwood Eddy, who travelled the world over as a YMCA evangelist, states, "The hard core of sin consists of making ourselves the center of life." He then goes on to point out that most destructive sins arise from this core (1954:231).

Growth in Christian stewardship entails moving from self-centeredness into God-centeredness, drowning the self in the love of God and immersing the ego in the will of God.

James and John once asked Jesus for the privilege to be second and third in command when Christ's empire was established, sitting one at Christ's right hand and the other at his left in his "glory."

For displaying such ambition, they were cut short by the Master who told them:

> *You do not know what you are saying. He then asked, Are you able to drink the cup I drink and be baptized with the baptism with which I am baptized?* (Mk 10:35-40).

Jesus wanted them to examine themselves to see if they were ready to go with him along the bloody path he was taking. James soon did take that way, for it is recorded in Acts 12:2 that Herod *"killed James, the brother of John, with the sword."* Tradition has it that John also made the supreme sacrifice for his master.

The only way that we can serve God is to directly or indirectly serve our neighbors who are in need. We must follow Christ's example who said he had come:

> *. . . to preach good news to the poor . . . to proclaim release to the captives and recovering of sight to the blind, to set at liberty those who are oppressed* (Lk 4:18).

The Spirit which led Jesus to so serve is the same Spirit that dwells in Christ's people today (see Rm 8:15-17).

For anyone who does not have interest in learning how to serve neighbors, near and far, in the spirit of Christ, the sovereignty of God is only a theory. To such a person God is not truly acknowledged as lord. The faith of such a person will have a hard time to survive.

In his parables, Jesus most often pictured his would-be followers as servants. And the earliest recorded command of Jesus, given by way of his word to Satan in the wilderness of temptation, makes being a servant of God inseparable from worshiping God:

> *You shall worship the Lord your God and him only shall you serve* (Lk 4:8).

The corollary to the first basic principle of Christian stewardship — that God is the supreme ruler over all — is the second basic principle:

GOD HAS PLACED ALL PEOPLE ON EARTH TO BE GOD'S SERVANTS.

In *Markings,* Dag Hammarskjöld, who was secretary-general of the United Nations from 1953 to 1961, has penned a valuable prayer for those who desire to be faithful servants of God:

Give me a pure heart — that I may see Thee,
A humble heart — that I may hear Thee,
A heart of love — that I may serve Thee (p. 93).

3

God is the Creator, Sustainer and Owner of All

An airline poster displaying a variety of beautiful scenes of different timberland carried the caption: "MOST OF THESE FORESTS ARE MAN-MADE."

It is almost certain that many people cooperated with God in getting those woodlands to grow, but the person who chose those words to describe the scene was not a careful reader of the Bible.

Of old a psalmist sang:

> *The heavens are thine, the earth also is thine;*
> *the world and all that is in it, thou hast*
> *founded them* (Ps 89:11).

When the apostle Paul was witnessing to those skeptics in Athens and commenting on their precautionary altar for those who worshiped "AN UNKNOWN GOD," he declared he himself worshiped *"the God who made the world and everything in it"* (Ac 17:24).

The Bible contains myriad other similar statements.

Too often humans are inclined to claim excessive credit for the accomplishment of some good enterprise.

This is analogous to the flea on the back of the elephant. The pair crossed a small stream on a suspension bridge making it creak and swing wildly with every step taken. Reaching the opposite side safely, the flea opined to the elephant, "We certainly made that bridge shake, didn't we?"

Much of our gloating over our exploits is on a par with that flea's.

After a child had listened intently to her mother tell the creation story of the Bible, she asked her mother, "What has God been doing since?"

Her mother replied by explaining how God kept the sun shining, the earth making its rounds, the clouds dropping rain, plus all the trees and flowers and even the blades of grass growing. To that the lass responded, "I should think God would get tired and quit."

The parent countered, "My child, God is love and love never quits."

God is creator of all. What is more, God prizes all of creation and sustains it all.

A cynic once asked, "What has God done for me?"

The reply might have been: "God has done for you and continues to do for you more things than you can imagine — approximately 10,000 heartbeats a day, countless communications passing through billions of nerve centers and cells of your body daily, making it possible for you to function with greater complexity and efficiency than anything that the smartest human being can even envisage."

It is too easy to take all this sustaining love for granted and not acknowledge our moment-by-moment dependence on our Creator, our Sustainer and our Owner.

The New Testament deals mainly with how believers in the Savior belong, through God's saving grace, to God and it is for this reason that they should live for God. Paul put it succinctly:

> *You are not your own, you were bought with a price. So glorify God in your body* (1 Co 6:19, 20).

It is difficult to understand how God could sacrifice Jesus Christ, his only Son, to die on a cross in order to make it possible for us to be transformed from broken, sinful creatures into cleansed and whole persons who can eternally be one with the holy and majestic Sovereign of all. It is to this great God of power, glory, victory, majesty and love that we belong.

In *The Christian Doctrine of Creation and Redemption* Emil Brunner wrote:

> To affirm existence as God-given can mean nothing less than the recognition of our

existence as God's property and thus to dedicate it to him (p. 172).

Thus the third principle which should govern our thinking and practice of Christian stewardship is:

GOD IS THE CREATOR, SUSTAINER AND OWNER OF ALL.

4

All are God's Stewards

The word "steward" as it was generally understood in the time of Jesus' physical sojourn represented a trusted overseer of a household. Jesus once asked his disciples,

> *Who then is the faithful and wise steward whom his master will set over his household?*
> (Lk 12:42).

When this question, and Jesus' parable in which it is found, was being considered by a group of church leaders, one of them volunteered the following illustration: "One hot midday a man was stretched out in the shade of a tree to sleep. When he was disturbed by a fly, he ordered his pet monkey who was beside him to keep the fly away. A fly lit on the man's nose. The monkey killed it with a stone, badly bruising his master's nose." The narrator added, "The monkey was faithful but not wise."

When the laughter subsided the narrator asked: "Aren't there sometimes stewards like that?" Heads nodded.

In one of Jesus' parables two servants accepted their stewardship responsibility differently. One misused his master's goods, some of it for personal satisfaction, even getting intoxicated. He also misused authority that was entrusted to him, beating fellow-servants. When the master returned, that servant was given a beating and dismissed.

On the other hand the faithful servant who did what was expected during the master's absence was rewarded when the day of settlement arrived and even given more opportunities to enjoy even greater confidence of his master, plus the honor of high office and close contact with the good master (see Lk 12:42-46).

Such choices are given to all of us. Thus when Jesus was about to leave his disciples, shortly after his resurrection, he said to them, *"As the Father sent me, so I send you"* (Jn 20:21). He was sending them on a great mission, as God had sent him on a great mission. Theirs was to be a very high vocation. Similarly, ours as Christ's stewards, is a high vocation.

Defining his God-commissioned stewardship, Jesus once said,

> *For I have come down from heaven, not to do my own will, but the will of him who sent me*
> (Jn 6:38).

Faithful and wise stewardship requires hearts conquered by God's love and minds mastered by God's will. To be a steward of God is not an option for the Christian.
To the Christians of Corinth Paul wrote:

> *What have you that you did not receive?* (1 Co 4:7).

The apostle Peter wrote to believers scattered in many nations by persecution:

> *As each has received a gift, employ it for one another, as good stewards of God's varied grace* (1 P 4:10).

There are those who feel that such responsibility is too great. Some may say, "I am glad there are those who take the stewardship way, but I prefer to go along the way I am."

However, entrusted with life by the Eternal Creator, no such choice is open to any of us. All are stewards of God, faithful and wise, or unfaithful and unwise.

William Law, in *A Serious Call,* long ago wrote:

> We must do everything as servants of God,
> We must live in every place as in his presence,
> We must use everything as that ought to be used which belongs to God (p 51).

The fourth basic principle to guide us in our thinking and practice of Christian stewardship is:

THE CHRISTIAN IS GOD'S STEWARD, HOLDING LIFE AND ALL ELSE POSSESSED AS A TRUST FROM GOD.

5

Stewards are Accountable to God

The Gospel of Matthew relates to us Jesus' parable about the three servants who were entrusted with large sums of money by their master. The underlying point of that parable was that:

> . . . *after a long time the master of those servants came and settled accounts with them* (25:19).

This story is followed by Jesus' description of the people of all nations who are called before the Son of Man seated *"on his glorious throne"* to give account of the ways in which they have used what had been entrusted to them.

In this setting Jesus identified himself with the hungry, the thirsty, the naked, the sick and those in prison. Christ came to earth on a mission of compassion for those in need and spent much of his time preparing his followers for a similar mission.

The invitation to follow Christ was not a summons to an easy life, rather it was to come serve as Christ's yokemates.

The wise master keeps his servants aware of the fact that an account will need to be made of service rendered. Anticipating such accounting serves as an encouragement to promptness in service and to a high quality of work. The call to Christian stewardship is a call to a high vocation. It is not to be taken lightly. It needs to be matched with a high sense of accountability.

We saw in the apostle Paul's letter to the Ephesians that Christians are *"created in Christ Jesus for good works."* In the last book of the Bible are the words of the One who gave his life for the church saying,

And all the churches shall know that I am he who searches mind and heart and I will give to each of you as your works deserve (Rv 2:23).

Long before Jesus spent three years training the twelve, God's people were told in the book of Proverbs:

If you say, "Look, we did not know this," does not he who weighs the heart perceive it? Does not he who keeps watch over your soul know it? And will he not repay all according to their deeds? (24:12).

Once in a study session a parishioner asked, "If God is a parent who loves us dearly, explain why such a loving parent requires an accounting of us?" Should not an answer be that parents who truly love their children will help them become better performers by occasionally reviewing their work, correcting what needs to be corrected and commending what deserves commending?

God is not only Father. He is also Owner of all, the supreme Lord of all. God highly honors his servants by entrusting to them priceless treasures with which to render faithful and wise service.

Even though we may feel that some of the words of the following prayer were not well chosen, they are inspiring and must, nevertheless, have been helpful to the soldier who made the supreme sacrifice on a battlefield and in whose pocket they were found.

> Jesus, whose lot with us was cast,
> Who saw it out from first to last;
> Would that I could win and keep and feel
> That heart of love, that spirit of steel.
> I would not to your bosom fly
> To slink off 'til the storms go by.
> If you are like the man you were
> You'd turn in scorn from such a prayer,
> Flog me, spur me and set me straight
> At some vile job I'd fear and hate.
> Do you but keep me — hope or none —
> Cheery and staunch 'til all is done.
> —*Author unknown.*

The quality of Christian stewardship is certain to improve if the steward often looks to the Great Steward who himself *"endured the Cross and thought nothing of its shame because of the joy he knew would follow his suffering"* (Heb 12:3).

Inspiration can come by keeping before one this "heart of love," and "spirit of steel."

To anticipate giving final account of Christian stewardship to the great God of infinite love can always be a source of joy, as well as stimulation to better service.

The fifth basic principle to guide us in our thinking and practice of Christian stewardship is:

THE STEWARD OF THE ETERNAL SUPREME LORD WILL BE CALLED UPON TO GIVE AN ACCOUNT.

6

Faithful Stewards Serve Out of Gratitude

"I knew you to be a hard master," said the unfaithful one-talent steward.

Actually, his master was a kind man. Jesus points out that he highly rewarded the two stewards who were faithful in their use of the two and five talents that had been entrusted to them (see Mt 25:14-24).

One talent was a large sum. *The New Testament in Modern English* translation by J.B. Phillips makes the talent one thousand pounds, which at the time amounted to a few thousand dollars. No wonder the one-talent servant was regarded as ungrateful and a complete failure for with such resources he could have begun any number of ventures.

In the first chapter of Paul's letter to the Christians at Rome is found one of the longest lists of sins recorded in the Bible. Paul's preamble at the beginning says, *for although they knew God they did not honor him as God or give thanks to him, but they became futile in their thinking and their senseless minds were darkened* (v. 21).

We may conclude from this declaration that where gratitude is lacking, minds are not open to truth or to the light needed if we are to live for God and to serve God.

When the great prophet Samuel anointed Saul to be king over Israel he counseled the people:

Only fear the Lord and serve him faithfully with all your heart, for consider what great things he has done for you (1 S 12:24).

Bountiful blessing from God was powerful motivation for whole-hearted service to God, in Samuel's view.

We have much greater reason than had those Israelites to give thought to God's goodness for we have had countless blessings of which they could know nothing because the Savior came to the world.

   His glorious teachings.
   His tireless labors for us.
   His dying on a cross for us.
   His rising, victor over sin and death for us.
   His welcoming us as His brethren.
   His promise of a resplendent eternal home.
   His love poured into our hearts by the Holy
      Spirit.

His presence with us, to guide, strengthen
and cheer us.

His gift of happy fellowship with other redeemed friends.

His other innumerable unspeakable blessings.

If Christ in physical form were to come to our homes, we would want to do many things for him, with all our hearts and strength. We would provide him a comfortable place to rest. We would give of the very best that we have to refresh him. We would want to know if there were errands we could run for him. This we would want to do for him because he has done and is doing so many things for us.

Paul's sense of indebtedness to God for his new life in Christ made him an immensely fruitful steward of God's grace. Deep gratitude impelled him in daring and untiring service for his Redeemer —

> ... *in afflictions, hardships, calamities, beatings, imprisonments, tumults, labors, hunger*
> (2 Co 6:4-5).

Before Paul and after him, many have made the supreme sacrifice for their Lord. As they faced their persecutors their spirit has been:

You can kill us with stones,
You can cut us down with the sword,
You can feed us to wild beasts,
You can nail us to crosses,

> You can burn us at the stake,
> You can pull our bodies apart, limb by limb,
> We would rather so die for him than live without him.

Even in this century, out of loving gratitude, more faithful servants of our gracious Lord have endured privations and suffering — *"even unto death"* — than in any other century.

Gratitude to God opens the mind to receive more light and expands the heart to receive more of God's love which does much to generate faithful, wise and joyous Christian stewardship.

The sixth principle to guide us in our thinking and practice of Christian stewardship is:

THE FAITHFUL CHRISTIAN STEWARD SERVES GOD UNRESERVEDLY OUT OF GRATITUDE FOR GOD'S BOUNTIFUL GIVING.

7

The Great Purpose of Christian Stewardship is to Glorify God

A church choir director asked a clerk in a music store for a copy of an anthem with the title, "The Glory of the Lord." The clerk called to the person working in the storage shelves for a copy. Finding none, that clerk called down: " 'The Glory of the Lord' is out of print."

In print and in thought, the Shekinah Glory of our Lord does not have the prominence nor attention it should have.

It was when young Isaiah became profoundly aware of the glory of God, as he saw him *"upon a throne, high and lifted up,"* that he was stirred to discover the divine purpose for his life, setting him on his way to become the greatest prophet after Moses and one who would counsel and rebuke princes and kings.

The pronouncement which so moved him was:

Holy, holy, holy is the Lord of hosts;

the whole earth is full of his glory.

When Isaiah felt the foundation of the temple tremble, this so humbled him that he fell down and cried,

Woe is me! For I am a man of unclean lips and I dwell in the midst of a people of unclean lips; for my eyes have seen the King, the Lord of hosts! (6:3-5).

Before Solomon built the temple in Jerusalem, his father King David had the Ark of the Covenant that contained the two stone tablets on which were engraved the Ten Commandments brought there.

The Ark was the symbol of the presence of God. When the Ark was first placed in the tabernacle in Jerusalem many offerings were made. Then a long hymn of thanksgiving was sung with the chorus accompanied by a large instrumental band. In the hymn were the lines:

*Declare his glory among the nations . . .
Ascribe to the Lord the glory due to his name*
(1 Ch 16:24, 29).

The words, *"Ascribe to the Lord the glory due to his name"* appears many times in the Psalms.

When an angel announced the birth of Jesus to the shepherds, Scripture tells that suddenly *"a multitude of the heavenly host"* joined the angel and added: *"Glory to*

God in the highest." Heaven was proclaiming that the purpose of Jesus' coming to the earth was to glorify God.

Very early in his teaching those who would follow him, Jesus said,

> *Let your light so shine before others, so that they may see your good works and give glory to your Father in heaven* (Mt 5:16).

And then during his last meal with his disciples before he was crucified, Jesus told them there in the Upper Room that the proof of their being considered his disciples would be seen in their bearing fruit that would glorify God (Jn 15:8).

In that same discourse, and in the only long prayer of Jesus that has been recorded, he summarized his entire ministry with the words,

> *I glorified thee on the earth, having accomplished the work thou gavest me to do* (Jn 17:4).

In the letter that the apostle Peter wrote to the Christians scattered far by persecutions he told them that they should serve as good stewards *"in order that in everything god may be glorified"* (1 P 4:11).

To glorify God is to proclaim God's nature — God's holiness, God's love, God's power, and more, as it is revealed in the Holy Scriptures and in the life of Jesus. This is to be done by our life, by our deeds and by our words.

The late Bishop William Temple of London, in *Nature, Man and God,* has said,

> The true aim of the soul is not its own salvation; to make that the chief aim is to ensure its perdition; for it is to fix the soul on itself as center. The true aim of the soul is to glorify God (pp. 390-391).

In our missionary service, my wife and I have been privileged to share in the worship of God with people of many countries, of many tribes. The hymn that we have heard enthusiastically sung on all corners of the globe has been the one that bears the title, "How Great Thou Art." Over and over, around the world, we have heard this hymn sung with exuberant enthusiasm.

Why should this be? Is it not because the words of the hymn point to the greatness of God as Creator of all, as the loving suffering Redeemer and as the Heavenly Father who provides an eternal home? These words cause hearts to overflow with gratitude and a desire to praise and glorify our great and loving God.

For many of God's people the unparalleled passages in the last book of the Bible are the great celebration choruses, where we read of:

> *the mighty voice of a great multitude in heaven, crying: "Hallelujah! Salvation and glory and power belong to our God"* (Rv 19:1; see also 4:9-11, 5:12, 7:12 and 19:7).

The seventh and final basic principle of Christian stewardship that we note to guide us in our thinking and practice of Christian stewardship is:

THE GREAT PURPOSE OF CHRISTIAN STEWARDSHIP IS THAT GOD WILL BE GLORIFIED IN EVERYTHING.

And when considering the basic principles of Christian stewardship, nothing sums them up better than the magnificent benediction found at the end of the Epistle of Jude:

> *Now to him who is able to keep you from falling and to present you without blemish before the presence of his glory with rejoicing, to the only God, our Savior through Jesus Christ our Lord be glory, majesty, dominion and authority, before all time and now and forever. Amen*

Part 2

Four Major Stewardship

Responsibilities

8

The Highest Stewardship Responsibility is for the Gospel

Traditionally, major stewardship responsibilities have been referred to in terms of three "T"s — Time, Talent and Treasure.

A fourth "T" should head the list. Truth by which all humankind can be set free. *"You will know the truth,"* said Jesus, *"and the truth will make you free"* (Jn 8:32).

Truth that the Bethlehem angel declared to the shepherds was *"good news of great joy which will come to all the people"* (Lk 2:10).

This good news of great joy, as described by Paul, is *"the power of God for salvation to everyone who has faith"* (Rm 1:16). And it is great joy for this power can liberate from sin which wounds, burdens, saddens, imprisons and destroys. This divine power that heals, lifts away great burdens, gladdens, sets life free and makes people whole.

The most often referred to parable of Jesus tells of such an experience of great joy — the home-coming of the "prodigal son." Jesus explains that the rejoicing father revealed the reason for his joy: *"My son was dead and is alive again!"* (Lk 15:24).

And this theme continues throughout the New Testament. Paul wrote to the new believers in Ephesus, *"You, he made alive when you were dead through trespasses and sins in which you once walked"* (Ep 2:1). Is it any wonder that elsewhere Paul spoke of this good news as *"the glorious gospel"* (1 Tm 1:11).

This resuscitation from a state of the living dead to a vital aliveness in Christ Jesus is what countless others who have experienced it and lived by it, know it to be. And many describe this in testimony and songs of praise such as these lines of the modern writer who was freed and made alive by this glorious gospel:

> Out of my bondage, sorrow and night,
> Into Thy freedom, gladness and light,
> Out of my sickness into Thy health,
> Out of my sin and into Thyself,
> Jesus, I come to Thee.
> —*William T. Sleeper*

One Sunday morning in a small mountain-slope church in the Philippines 23 people were received into membership of the church. After the worship service a friend said to the pastor, "It must be a great joy for you to have such good results from your labors!"

The pastor nodded but then explained, "In reality, it has been the work of one member in this church who has won to Christ 17 of the 23. He's sitting alone in the last row, by the door."

My friend approached the elderly man sitting in the back with a face beaming with joy and said to him, "Your pastor just told me that you brought 17 of these new members to Christ."

He nodded, "Yes, God has blessed my going to their homes to read the Bible and pray with them."

Just then my friend noticed that one of the old man's legs was twice as large as the other. Obviously he was suffering from elephantiasis. Astonished, he asked him, "But have you been going up and down these rough mountain trails here to visit these people with that leg?"

Still smiling, the man replied, "Oh yes, God gives me strength to drag it along."

"You must go to the hospital to get that leg attended to," my friend counseled.

Quickly came the response, "Yes, I plan to do that soon, but first I am waiting for three more families that I am visiting to come to the Lord."

Obviously it was more important to this infirm gentleman to risk his own health in order to be able to share this revitalizing glorious Gospel with his neighbors who were still in bondage and sorrow.

When Paul instructed Titus to shepherd the new believers carefully in his stead, he urged him to help them *"show entire and true fidelity, so that in everything they may adorn the doctrine of God our Savior"* (Tt 2:10).

In other words, they were to make the doctrine attractive to others so that they would joyfully leave their bondage and sorrow and find freedom and gladness in Christ.

Once at the close of a seminar we were giving, an enthusiastic participant invited us to join him on a walk to his village to encourage the newly formed Christian fellowship there. This new group regularly worshiped in the home of the police chief.

When we arrived at the police chief's house, the word went around and soon we were holding a brief worship service. We noted that on one side of the house there was a large pile of freshly sawed lumber. It was explained this would soon be used for the framework of a small church they were planning to build.

Not long before this, the pregnant wife of the police chief had died. Traditionally the non-Christian women of the village refused to touch the body of anyone deceased to prepare it for burial, because it was their belief that to do so meant that all subsequent childbirths in their families would be stillborn.

When the police chief's wife died, however, the few Christian women of the village ignored this taboo and performed this dreaded ministry, proclaiming to him by their good deeds their freedom from the bondage and sorrow of their old bans.

The good works of the Christian women in this village had broken down the barriers to God's love in the mind and heart of the police chief and now the soul of this grieving man had been made alive through this glorious gospel. He had been brought to believe and to love God with all his heart, soul, mind and strength because of this simple, good deed.

Now the police chief, in turn, was also performing good works for he was helping to build a small church where many others would be able to hear the Good News, the Eternal Truth, and where they could worship happily and serve the God who gives life to those who were once dead in bondage to sin.

All Christian stewards can share in witnessing for Christ in the most convincing way. Non-believers, skeptics and those who oppose the Christian faith are drawn to Christ when the truth that makes you free is seen in the good works of Christ's followers.

It was so in the first Christian century as it is today. This was most strikingly seen when Saul of Tarsus, the killer of Christians, saw Stephen praying for those who were in the process of stoning him to death. The amazing growth of the church in China in recent years is an inspiring modern evidence of a similar response to the good works of those who follow Christ in the face of martyrdom.

Such behavior is to be expected from those who have been made alive in Christ Jesus and is the direct result of one of the last promises Jesus made to his disciples:

> *I am the vine, you are the branches. Those who abide in me and I in them bear much fruit* (Jn 15:5).

Thus the primary goal of all Christian stewardship must be bearing much fruit — proclaiming the good news of life in Christ Jesus to those in deathly bondage to sin. It is a special source of joy and strength for those who witness to realize that God, who is love, is the source of life for witness, for by abiding in the Branch which is Christ, we have access to power and great service as described in the words of our Savior's Great Commission:

> *All authority in heaven and on earth has been given to me. Go therefore and make disciples of all nations, baptizing them in the name of the Father and the Son and the Holy Spirit, teaching them to observe all that I have commanded you; and lo, I am with you always, to the close of the age* (Mt 28:18, 19).

9

Stewardship Responsibility for Time

Once in Guyana, South America, my wife and I were having breakfast with a local pastor and his wife in their delightful tropical setting. We commented on what a lovely spot of the earth they had surrounding them.

The pastor began telling us how he had been awakened long before sunrise a few mornings earlier by noises from among the banana plants below their bedroom window. The next day he had asked the church and school gardener if he happened to know what had been going on among the banana plants at that early hour.

"I was watering them," said the gardener.

"At 3:00 A.M.!" the pastor exclaimed, adding, "That's an ungodly hour to be watering plants!"

"Pastor," retorted the gardener, "Are there any ungodly hours? Aren't they all his?"

Our host admitted that the rebuke was timely. The gardener had given a splendid interpretation of Psalm 74:16

Thine is the day, thine also is the night.

The Psalms are full of reminders that should help us avoid thinking that the hours as well as the days are not our own to be used as we please.

This is the day which the Lord has made; let us rejoice and be glad in it. (118:24)

We gave a stewardship seminar once in India attended by a physician who had a large private practice in his own city. A few months after he had returned home he wrote me a letter which said, "Since I was at the stewardship seminar more than 50 of my patients have left my office with Psalm 118:24 as part of my prescription for them."

A vast number of people have found that to acknowledge that every day is a precious gift from God contributes to their physical well-being as well as to their spiritual well-being.

If the Christian steward is to carry out the Great Commission faithfully, much thought must be given to the good stewardship of time — much more than is usually given this topic by the people of God.

In many lands such expressions as "Time is gold," or "One pound of gold won't buy one moment of time," are proverbial. Yet many people do not highly prize the time entrusted to them.

If we were to stop and do a bit of calculation, it might help us to keep a useful overview of the subject. Should on the average in an adult lifetime, an hour a day is wasted, in 40 years it would add up to 14,600 hours. That is 1,825 eight-hour working days, or almost seven years of working days.

In his letters to the Christians at Ephesus and at Colossae Paul wrote: *"Make the most of time."* In another letter he also states that the person who does not use time well is:

- Like a sleeper.
- Like a dead person.
- In the dark.
- Unwise.
- Lacking understanding of what the will of the Lord is (see Ep 5:14-17).

Many who make no pretense of living for God misuse their weekends as well as other time entrusted to them by God in questionable kinds of behavior either motivated by desires for self-indulgence or for self-aggrandizement.

If all those who bear the honorable name of the crucified Savior would use a reasonable amount of time in learning better to use this valuable gift of God, much more would be done to bring in the Kingdom of God — the acceptance of God's reign.

It is in the use of time that we all have opportunity to give God first place. Jesus made that clear early in his training of his disciples, *"Seek first God's kingdom and his righteousness"* (Mt 6:33) — our time must be devoted first of all to what is right in God's sight.

Truly, "God First!" is a good motto to follow in all of life.

Even as a lad of twelve, Jesus showed much appreciation for the great value of time. Thus he questioned his parents when they had been searching for him in the Jerusalem temple area for three days: *"Wist ye not that I must be about my Father's business?"* (Lk 2:48.)

In his love, God has plans for the use of time. Following them will always be beneficial for us and will contribute to fulfilling God's purpose in the world.

10

Stewardship Responsibility for Talent

In an undeveloped interior area of Colombia, South America, a group of Christians was permitted to settle on so-called "waste lands." Their new village was called Nasaret. When we were visiting there, a doctor who worked in the clinic told us of the characteristic Christian acts of some of the townspeople.

Once a lad came down from a mountain valley and urgently reported that all the other members of his family were very ill and badly in need of medical attention. The doctor and the pastor with the local congregation quickly arranged for men from the village to go to the mountain valley carrying poles and blankets with which to bring back the sick to the clinic. Because the doctor suspected that the family was suffering from a contagious disease, the women of the church volunteered to clean an abandoned hut which could serve the ill family as a quarantine area.

Soon the men returned with their burdens, weary from their long trek but happy with the expectation that these sick neighbors would recover. For many weeks, day and night, women of the congregation plus the lad who had escaped his family's fate, tended the sick under the direction of the doctor.

Is it any wonder that the recovered family was soon sharing in the joyous worship of God and in a variety of services rendered by the congregation? The chain reaction of divine love demonstrated by the members was not surprising.

It has been fascinating for us to chart the subsequent study programs which we held in that region, for we noted that we have had fellowship with friends —

- of a church in San Pedro that grew out of the church at Nasaret,
- of a church at San Vicente that grew out of the church in San Pedro,
- of a church at Mercado that grew out of the church at San Vicente,
- of a church at Tulapa that grew out of the church at Mercado.

In that region there are now more than 40 churches united together who work for Christ's continuing mission in programs of education, healing, self-help and witnessing. As they strive to be channels of the truth about God's love, they find their churches multiplying.

In one of the lists of persons who have gifts which have been obviously received from God with which to render service, Paul includes *"helpers"* (1 Co 12:28).

Perhaps none of the dozen or more carriers who bore that sick family down to that Colombian clinic nor any of the women who helped care for them in their contagious state, was known as a "talented person," yet with their "helper-talents" this community of believers made it possible for a family to be restored to health. And in the process they helped to set in motion acts of mercy that continue to bear fruit to this day.

Persons of special talent are often spoken of as "being gifted" because it is generally acknowledged that such talented persons have not earned their special abilities.

To those who were not humble enough to acknowledge this gift, Paul wrote: *"What have you that you did not receive? If then you received it, why do you boast as if it were not a gift?"* (see 2 Co 4:7).

As God's good stewards, each one of us with varying kinds of abilities, we are not only to do good deeds frequently, we are at all times to live our stewardship for God, whether as Christian teachers, as Christian students, as Christian nurses, as Christian doctors, as Christian office-workers, as Christian farmers, as Christian architects, as Christian home-keepers or as Christian workers of any sort.

Paul, who showed himself to be a very faithful steward of God, wrote *"Whatever your task, work heartily serving the Lord"* (Col 3:23). With this understanding of Christian stewardship, quality of work will be high and satisfaction gotten from it great.

Any wise owner of a costly and delicate instrument takes good care of it. What more valuable instruments can we have than our own bodies? Thus the faithful and wise steward of God will take good care of it, not only because that body is delicate and irreplaceable, but also because it is a trust from God.

To indulge in habits that are harmful to the body is an offense to God. Since Scriptures refer to the body as a temple of God (1 Co 6:19), to do anything harmful to our bodies is tantamount to vandalizing the House of God.

During the Crimean War an army nurse was caring for a severely wounded soldier from the opposing army. When the soldier was fully on the way to recovery he learned that the brother of this nurse had been killed by the troops of his army. When he asked the nurse, "How could you do so much to save my life when we killed your brother?" she replied: "It is not I, but Jesus working through me."

> Through the life of the Christian God lives.
> Through the heart of the Christian God loves.
> Through the voice of the Christian God speaks.
> Through the hands of the Christian God serves.

11

Stewardship Responsibility for Treasure

Students of a high school English class were assigned to write essays on "Science and Religion." One turned in an essay that began: "Science is material, religion is immaterial."

Since early days of recorded human history there have been religious and non-religious writers who have considered the sacred and the secular to have little, if anything, in common.

Once a pastor who attended our stewardship seminars said that when he left home, an officer of his church said to him, "Pastor, greet the visiting speaker. Tell him to talk about spiritual things, like prayer and Bible study."

Such thinking tends to ignore the vast amount the Bible has to say about material things and about the contributions that the material can make to a wholesome spiritual experience.

Thus we read, *"Be glad and rejoice for ever in that which I create"* (Is 65:18). *"Honor the Lord with your substance . . ."* (Pr 3:9) and *"For where your treasure is there will your heart be also"* (Mt 6:21).

In this last passage Jesus was pointing out that where material investment is made, personal commitment follows.

A woman we knew who belonged to a small church had long prayed that her husband would join her in worshiping there. The congregation had no musical accompaniment for singing the hymns and was very eager to acquire a small organ. The non-member husband heard about this problem and decided to contribute the amount needed for the purchase of the organ. Of course, he was present for its dedication and from then on he regularly attended the worship services until finally he became an active member of the church. His heart had followed his treasure.

The Gospel is quick to point out that those who are not faithful stewards of material things cannot experience spiritual graces deeply. Jesus said: *"If then you have not been faithful in unrighteous mammon, who will entrust to you the true riches?"* (Lk 16:11).

In our culture we are much attached to material things and are all dependent on material things every moment, waking or sleeping. From this stance it is a slippery and easy step to regard material things as the most important elements in our life. That is likely why the Bible has so much in it about material things; including warnings against becoming too attached to them. In fact, in a list of evils that Paul said should be *"put to death,"* he included covetousness which he called *"idolatry"* (Col 3:5).

Jesus apparently considered the warning against being possessed by material things so important that he repeatedly gave striking illustrations to emphasize the warning such as the story of the landowner who decided to build bigger barns to accommodate a burgeoning harvest, but who did not live a day in which to enjoy them (Lk 12:13-21).

Another time Christ told of the wealthy man, *"dressed in purple,"* who had ignored the plight of his poor neighbors. From the flames of hell, he implored the far-off Abraham to send the one-time beggar, Lazarus, just to moisten his burning tongue with a finger-tip of water (Lk 16:19-31).

The renowned author, Rev. George A. Buttrick of New York City, once began an address to a gathering in Manila with a quote clipped from the *Wall Street Journal,* "The lure of quick money has killed more people than ever fell on the battlefield." Who better to know the validity of such a statement than readers of this journal who are regular watchers of the New York Stock Exchange reports.

The ever increasing number of modern consumer goods available in our country for our pleasure, convenience and profit has turned our generation into a more materialistic society than that of preceding generations.

An African scholar when asked how she would differentiate the White race from the Black race, replied, "The White race has. The Black race is." Surely this emphasis on the materialistic is born out by the bumper sticker seen by a visitor to Southern California which says, "I SHOPPED, THEREFORE I AM."

It was probably because he had learned of mounting materialism in some members of the church at Philippi that Paul, in his letter to them, included a warning for those among them who lavishly indulge *"in earthly things."* He went on to assert that being involved in such indulgence was to *"live as enemies of the cross of Christ"* (see Ph 3:18, 19).

A major cause of the economic crises and the conflicts the world over is greed. There is still need of the warning given long ago by Oliver Goldsmith:

> Ill fares the land, to hastening ills a prey
> when wealth accumulates and men decay.

Greed usurps devotion to God, destroys peace in human relationships and leads to untold suffering by the impoverishment of people throughout the world.

Stewardship of material treasure includes responsibility for the physical environment. Stewards of God are to be environmental stewards. The destruction of the physical environment should alarm the child of the God who is creator of all.

Streams and lakes are being choked. Rivers, wells and oceans are being polluted. The atmosphere is poisoned by toxic acids and its ozone depleted. Vast lands are stripped of their forests. Some regions are becoming barren because of over-grazing, others are rendered odious by masses of garbage. A current newspaper account tells of residents at the outskirts of a city seeing less of the sunsets because of the rising garbage dump that is obstructing their view.

God's first instruction to the human creature was to care for his physical creation. In that great worship book of the Bible, The Psalms, nature has a very prominent place. The singer of one of the last recorded psalms tells of God being praised by the sun, moon and stars, fire, hail, snow and frost, sea monsters, fir trees and cedars, mountains and hills, beasts and cattle, creeping things and flying birds (148).

Jesus showed great appreciation of nature, referring in his teaching to the soil, water, clouds, birds, grasses, trees and much more of the earth's rich store. If we do not respect God's creation, how can we have respect for the Creator? Psalm 19, as well as other passages of the Bible, make it clear that nature exists to glorify God.

Decent people would never destroy, or even disfigure, those beautiful and irreplaceable works of art produced by great artists down through the ages. To damage such is considered reprehensible vandalism ascribable only to the deranged. Yet it is even more disgraceful to deliberately and unnecessarily damage the good earth.

God's stewards not only have a responsibility for preserving all creation, they also must share in cooperative efforts through all possible avenues to prevent waste, pollution and the plunder of natural resources. How bleak the recent warning from the Worldwatch Institute sounds: "Decisions we make today will quite literally determine the habitability of the world in which our children live."

>   Wise stewards keep learning more of God's
>   will for all that he has created.
>   Faithful stewards serve God increasingly well
>   with all that God has entrusted to them.
>   Devout stewards have respect for God's creation
>   and find joy in preserving it and using it as
>   good stewards,
>   for God's glory and the well-being of others.

Part 3

The Christian Steward

As a Giver

Introduction

When serving as evangelistic missionaries in China my wife and I first resided in Shanghai. The pastor of a very large church was the program committee chair of an evening discussion group that represented many churches. This group met periodically in the city's YMCA and one night he arranged for me to meet with the group. I chose for our theme: "The Christian and Money."

Among those present were a school principal, two gold-brokers and a doctor who was reputed to be the top surgeon of the city. The usual adjournment was at 9:00 P.M., but it was past 10:00 P.M., when we dispersed. The highly regarded doctor then said to me, "I know you came by tram. Let me take you home."

As we set off the surgeon said, "I'd like to talk with you some more about the subject of our discussion this evening. Some things you said are very revolutionary to me, especially your statement that 'For the Christian, giving is a spiritual matter more than it is a financial transaction.' So you'll know better why that struck me so hard, let me explain."

He began to describe what his regular church connection was and added: "Recently we made an addition to our church building to which I contributed quite a lot.

Beyond this I gave a substantial amount of money each month to help with the many war refugee camps resulting from the Japanese military occupation."

He listed other generous contributions he had made and then added, "But all these have been purely financial transactions. If there has been anything spiritual about them all, it has been on the debit side for when I total the amount up at the end of the year, I proudly say to myself, 'I doubt anyone else in Shanghai gives as much as I do.' I'm ashamed of myself. You don't know what a difference this evening's discussion is going to make for me."

To think that an hour or two of discussing that theme could, under God, make such a difference to a highly skilled professional made me plunge into a study of Christian giving more seriously than ever I had.

There is much in the Bible about God as a giver and also much of it has to do with God's people as givers. Jesus added significantly to the subject. Perhaps his most easily remembered words about it are: *"Freely ye have received, freely give"* (Mt 10:8). The Gospel record by Mark relates that Jesus once *"sat down opposite the treasury [of the temple] and watched the multitude putting money into the treasury"* (Mk 12:41). Obviously this was a matter of serious concern to Christ.

Thus the remainder of this volume will deal with first, general biblical instruction about giving; second, motives for giving; and third, the results for the stewards of God who are faithful and wise in this stewardship.

12

General Biblical Instructions

Question One. *Is any person bypassed in the invitation to give?*

Much of the worship of God as it is described in the early pages of the Bible took place in religious festivals; especially in the three great annual thanksgiving festivals of God's people. They were known as The Feast of the Passover, The Feast of First Fruits and The Feast of Tabernacles (also called The Harvest Festival).

Each festival lasted a week. All males twelve years and over were to participate in them in Jerusalem. The detailed attendance instructions included these words: *"None shall appear before me empty-handed"* (Ex 23:15 and other). Fruits, grains, unblemished animals and other produce were to be presented as offerings in the thanksgiving worship.

The first Christian churches, established in Ephesus, Corinth and elsewhere in the Roman world, participated in famine relief. When the apostle Paul wrote to the believers at Corinth about this he said: *"On the first day of the week each of you is to put something aside."* (1 Co 16:2). Another time Paul wrote to the people in these same churches about the believers of Macedonia (Philippi and others of the region), who in spite of their extreme poverty, had given *"beyond their means"* (2 Co 8:2,3).

Did that impoverish them? It seems not to have. The apostle wrote that out of *"abundance of joy [they were] begging us earnestly for the favor of taking part in the relief of the saints"* (2 Co 8:4).

How could that be? The first words that Paul wrote about their giving reveals the secret: *"We want you to know, brothers and sisters, about the grace of God that has been granted to the churches of Macedonia"* (2 Co 8:1). Their hearts were open to God's grace. True divine grace — giving — moves on to others.

Have you ever wondered how Jesus, with his great compassion for the poor, did not stop the poor widow who was giving her last two copper coins at the temple treasury? Why didn't he make one of the rich persons give for her? (see Lk 12:41-44). Could it have been that he saw fulfillment of the prayer of Hannah echoed by his mother in the Magnificat: *"He has filled the hungry with good things and the rich he has sent empty away"*? (Lk 1:53).

During a seminar I was giving in South America, a question was raised about the very poor being asked to give. My interpreter volunteered an illustration from his church. When the annual offering pledges were being passed out, a very poor woman was bypassed. She reached out for a pledge card, calling out loudly: "Have I received no blessings from God?"

Everyone in the faith community should have the opportunity to express gratitude to God for blessings received and in doing so be further blessed to become channels of blessing to others.

Another time when an usher was giving out the annual offering pledge cards he bypassed a group of young people. Later when asked why he did not give them pledge cards, he replied, "They are students and have no jobs." When asked if he believed that the young people paid for Friday evening tickets for their school basketball games or sometimes bought soft drinks, he said, "Of course they do."

This person had failed to realize that parents who are devoted church members would be happy to have their children develop the practice of participating in the offerings during Sunday worship.

Question Two. *What quality of gifts is suitable?*

A little girl and her younger brother came home from Sunday school where the lesson had been about Noah's ark.

"Let's play Noah and the ark," said little Anne.

"Good idea!" exclaimed little John, "Let's do the part when they landed on dry ground and made an offering."

Soon stones were arranged for the altar.

Anne asked, "What will we put on the altar?"

"Your old toy kitten," said John.

"No! Your dog," said Anne.

"No, we won't," exclaimed John.

Finally, another proposal made by Anne was agreeable — a little old goat. She explained, "We don't play with that any more. It's horns are broken and its tail is gone."

Too often it is what can be easily spared that is given.

But Scripture gives clear direction about what can serve as a suitable offering to God:

- *Abel brought of the firstlings and their fat portions* (Gn 4:4). (In other words, Abel brought the choicest parts.)
- *And Noah took of every clean animal and of every clean bird [the uninjured] and offered burnt offerings* (Gn 8:20).
- *The first of the first fruits of the ground you shall bring into the house of the Lord your God* (Ex 23:19).
- *Honor the Lord with your substance and with the first fruits of all your produce* (Pr 3:9).

It cannot be said too often that only the best that we have is good enough for God who is the Almighty. Both in worship and in service, gifts of little value to the worshiper are not really offerings to the Giver of All. Malachi dramatically states that such giving is an act of despising God.

Only by giving what is highly valued can worshipers evidence that they know God, the majestic Ruler and Giver of All. We cannot be in happy communion with the

Sovereign Lord unless we gladly render God the homage that is due the great King of Glory.

A pastor of a church in Bombay, India, told me the story of a child whose giving was much different from that portrayed by Anne and John and that of the Jerusalem worshipers of whom Malachi wrote. One Christmas Eve the church program ended with the children going forward placing gifts at a manger-scene — "gifts for Jesus." All participated except for one little girl who watched the proceedings intently, but showed no apparent unhappiness in having no gift to present.

At the early Christmas Day service this same little girl arrived at church with her parents but before taking her seat in the pew with her parents, she marched to the manger-scene and placed a nicely wrapped package there.

After the service the pastor's wife asked the child why she had delayed until morning to place her gift in the manger. With a radiant smile the girl responded, "I wanted to wait to choose the best gift I received this Christmas to give to Jesus."

Question Three.   *What is a commendable attitude to have in giving?*

In the dedication prayer that King David offered before a multitude of his people after they had given a vast amount of gold, silver, precious stones, choice woods and much else for the building of the magnificent temple in Jerusalem, he included this question: *"Who am I and what is my people that we should be able thus to offer willingly? For all things come from thee and of thine own have we given thee"* (1 Ch 29:14).

The very thought that such offerings would be accepted by the God of *"greatness, power, glory, victory and majesty"* seemed to astonish David. He did not ask God for more blessings to compensate for their generous outpouring. Rather he thanked and praised God that these gifts were acceptable.

Another time when David was in the countryside, he offered to buy a farmer's threshing floor so he could build an altar for making a sacrifice to God. The farmer replied, *"Let my lord and king take and offer up what seems good to him; here are the oxen for the burnt offering and the threshing sledges and the yokes of the oxen for the wood."*

But David protested: *"No, but I will buy it of you for a price; I will not offer burnt offerings to the Lord my God which cost me nothing"* (see 2 S 24:18-24).

When people are growing in knowledge of God it is for them a joy and an honor to worship the Lord with costly offerings. They do not ask, "Why must we give?" Their giving reminds me of the worshipers of two congregations where we gave seminars on Christian stewardship, concentrating on 1 Chronicles 29 and 2 Corinthians 8 and 9. Their pastors subsequently wrote us:

> We have a giving boom in our place now.
> —*Philippines*
>
> Our people are giving gold now — golden jewelry and plates. —*India*

Question Four. *To whom does the Christian give when giving according to the Holy Scriptures?*

As recorded in Exodus, the giving for the construction of the tabernacle in the wilderness, under the direction of Moses, was so abundant that the people were stopped in their giving (see Ex 36:1-7). One reason for the abundant giving of gold, silver, precious stones, fine wood, linen and other items needed was because Moses had asked that they bring offerings of these things *"to the Lord."*

Jesus said that when a person gives out of compassion for the needy, it is giving to him, showing him kindness. *"Truly I tell you, just as you did it to one of the least of these who are members of my family, you did it to me."* (Mt 25:40).

> Give as you would if an angel awaited your gift at the door;
> Give as you would if tomorrow were to find you where giving is o'er;
> Give as you would to the master if you met his searching look;
> Give as you would of his substance if his hand the offering took.
> —*Author unknown*

As we give, are we happy to think that Jesus looks upon our offering as he did the offerings he watched being made at the Jerusalem temple treasury?

Question Five. *What are some specific opportunities for giving?*

The Lord tells us the needy will always be with us. And we are right in hearing God spoken of as "the God of the poor" because of the many biblical references to God's compassion on the poor and the afflicted.

Thus the Lord responded sympathetically to the cries of the Hebrew slaves of Pharaoh (see Ex 2:23-25).

Later God instructed his people through Moses on how they should deal with the needy:

> *When you reap the harvest of your land, you shall not reap your field to its very border, neither shall you gather your gleanings after your harvest. And you shall not strip your vineyard bare, neither shall you gather the fallen grapes of your vineyard, you shall leave them for the poor and for the sojourner: I am the Lord your God* (Lv 19:9-10).

There is also instruction about lending to the poor: *"You shall not exact interest from them"* (Ex 22:25). God even explains his reason for such instruction: *"for I am compassionate"* (22:27).

Those going to the great annual festivals were told to go prepared to share food with widows and orphans (Dt 16:11).

In the Book of Psalms is a prayer for the king: *"May he defend the cause of the poor of the people, give deliverance to the needy"* (72:4).

In Proverbs we read: *"Those who oppress the poor insult their Maker, but those who are kind to the needy honor him"* (14:31).

The great prophet Isaiah challenged the selfish, pious oppressors of the poor: *"Is not this the fast that I choose . . . Is it not to share your bread with the hungry and bring the homeless poor into your house?"* (56:6-7).

In his ministry, the homeless Son of God was ever identifying himself with the poor. In a Nazareth synagogue when he first announced his purpose, Jesus proclaimed: *"The Spirit of the Lord is upon me, because he has anointed me to preach good news to the poor."* (Lk 4:18).

The first "official act" of the newly founded Church, soon after Pentecost, was the selection of seven deacons *"full of the Spirit and of wisdom"* to provide help for poor widows (see Ac 6:1-6).

Paul wrote to the Galatian Christians that when the church leaders in Jerusalem sent him and Barnabas to proclaim the Gospel to the Gentiles, the two of them were counseled to *"remember the poor, which very thing I was eager to do"* (Ga 2:10).

James, author of the little New Testament epistle bearing his name, emphasized the importance of having compassion on the poor. He said that if a person merely says to an ill-clad brother or sister who is lacking food, *"go in peace, be warmed and filled,"* that would be evidence that the speaker's faith is dead (see Jm 2:14-17).

Closely related to giving material aid to the poor is the need to provide justice for the poor. The prophet Jeremiah declared to his king: *"Thus says the Lord: 'Act with justice and righteousness and deliver from the hand of the oppressor anyone who has been robbed"* (Jr 22:3). In counseling the king about the importance of just dealings, he reminded him that his father, as king before him, *"judged the cause of the poor and needy,"* and added, *"Is not this to know me?"* (22:16). Unjustly treating the poor and needy is evidence of not knowing God.

The author of 1 John wrote that the Christian believer, who has something to share with a needy sister or brother, will inevitably share as evidence of God's love within (see 1 Jn 3:16-18).

A Gallup poll taken of the donations made by 2,775 persons in America revealed that those with comparatively larger annual incomes were not as generous as those with smaller incomes. One person commenting on this survey states that giving *"In America is a stark contrast* between heart-warming generosity and bone-chilling selfishness." It was found that households with annual incomes below $18,000 gave an average of 2.8 percent of their incomes whereas those with incomes between $50,000 and $75,000 gave 1.5 percent.[*]

The large amount of good left undone because of the lack of generosity by some who are able to give more is

---

[*] *Christian Century,* Nov. 2, 1989, p. 977.

appalling. No wonder Jesus' teaching contained much about the importance of generous giving, such as:

> *From everyone to whom much has been given, much will be required* (Lk 12:48).

When a rich man did not accept Jesus' challenge to be generous on behalf of the poor, Jesus said to his disciples:

> *Truly, I tell you, it will be hard for a rich person to enter the kingdom of heaven. Again I tell you, it is easier for a camel to go through the eye of a needle than for someone who is rich to enter the kingdom of God.*

When Jesus saw that those words shocked his disciples, he added: *"For mortals it is impossible, but for God all things are possible"* (see Mt 19:16-26).

Not only was Jesus indicating that aid to the needy is to have high priority in the benevolence lists of God's people, he was also saying that a good way to be rid of the addiction to wealth is to be generous in giving to the needy.

Today there is shocking destitution among the poor in many lands, including the U.S.A. as well as the necessity to remove the injustices that keep many imprisoned in their poverty.

Long before Jesus of Nazareth began to disturb the establishment in his day, God, through the prophet Micah, had informed his people what it meant *"to walk humbly with your God;"* namely: *"He has told you, O mortal, what is good; and what does the Lord require of you but to do justice and to love kindness"* (Mi 6:8).

A psalmist said that the one who hopes in God and keeps the faith, is the one *"who executes justice for the oppressed"* and *"who gives food to the poor"* (see Ps 146:5-7).

Question Six. *How is the amount given to be determined?*

In the Old Testament there is frequent reference to giving in terms of *"the tithe."* That is, from Abraham's giving of the tithe to Melchizedek the *"priest of God Most High"* (Gn 14:20) to the prophet Malachi's call to the people: *"Bring the full tithe into the storehouse"* (Ml 3:10).

The offering of the tithe was especially established to acknowledge God to be the owner of all, to honor God and to support the temple service of priests and Levites.

Worshipers were called upon to make many other offerings: of first-fruits (Ex 23:16), of first-born animals (Lv 27:26), thank-offerings and others (see Lv 7:12, 37 and Ex 29:39). In view of this we can assume that many gave much more than the tithe of their incomes.

In India a journalist who had been active in the Communist Party of his country was present at several sessions of a stewardship seminar. After the giving of the tithe had been discussed, he came to me and we had a long conversation.

One thing that seemed strange to him was that Christians were only asked to give a tenth of their income for

Christian causes. "As a Communist," he said, "I gave the party all except what I needed for bare necessities. Such was expected of me."

He went away pleased, as a new believer, to be assured that many Christians give much more than a tithe of their net incomes.

Another Old Testament guide for giving was stated in connection with the sharing to be done with the needy. During the three great thanksgiving festivals: *"All shall give as they are able, according to the blessing of the Lord your God"* (Dt 16:17).

It is interesting to note that what led Jesus to say to the tax collector, Zacchaeus, *"Today salvation has come to this house"* was that the renewal or re-birth of this man was evidenced by the first words out of this new convert's mouth: *"Behold, Lord, the half of my goods I give to the poor"* (Lk 19:8).

When Jesus was watching the *"rich people putting their gifts into the treasury"* and the poor widow putting in her *"two copper coins,"* Jesus commented: *"Truly, I tell you, this poor widow has put in more than all of them"* (Lk 21:1-4). Jesus was explaining that the measure of giving is determined by its costliness, the sacrifice made by the giver.

Matthew and Mark both tell of the woman who poured extravagant ointment on Christ's head which was valued at 300 denari, which was the equivalent of a year's wages of a vineyard worker of that time (see Mt 26:6-13 and Mk 14:3-9). Of this act, Jesus said, *"She has done a beautiful thing to me"* Mark 14:6 and prophesied that what she had done as an act of worship and service was so important it would be related together with the Gospel story throughout the world.

Paul, the great missionary apostle, advised new believers to give, with words reminiscent of Deuteronomy 16:17, *"according to the blessings of the Lord"* and reiterating what Jesus had said, *"From everyone to whom much has been given, much will be required"* (Lk 12:48) when he advised them, *"On the first day of every week, each of you is to put something aside and store it up, as he may propser"* (1 Co 16:2).

The amount to be given is not to be determined by sudden impulse. Rather, as Paul urged: *"Each of you must give as you have made up your mind"* (2 Co 9:7). He was saying that the amount to be given should be determined by carefully heeding instructions given.

13

Motives for Giving

If the reason for doing a commendable thing is not right, the result for the doer cannot be good, no matter how good the deed.

In the drama, *Murder in the Cathedral,* T.S. Eliot has Thomas à Becket say: "The last temptation is the greatest treason, to do the right thing for the wrong reason."

There is much in the Scripture teaching about those who give for the wrong reasons.

Wrong Motives

- *For self-glory*

Early in the "Sermon on the Mount" we have the words of Jesus: *"So whenever you give alms, do not sound a trumpet before you, as the hypocrites do in the synagogues and in the streets, so that they may be praised by others"* (Mt 6:2).

If the motive for giving is to gain praise, the giving is not worshiping God. It is not serving God. It is trying to use God for one's own benefit.

Once when I was visiting a church in Africa, the pastor announced from the pulpit the name of a member of the congregation, specifying the amount this congregant had recently given to the church. Later I asked the pastor if this was a common practice.

"Only when large amounts are given," was the reply.

This pastor was not remembering Jesus' appraisal of the varying amounts given, while he watched, at the treasury of the Jerusalem temple. Christ took time to sit and observe what was going on. His response to the many who gave large sums out of their riches and to the poor widow with her two copper coins was to call his disciples together to hear his important pronouncement:

Truly, I say to you, this poor widow has given more than all those who are contributing to the treasury (Mk 12:43).

We do not need to conclude that Jesus would object to all announcements about gifts that are given for he declared that the story of the woman's pouring the costly alabaster bottle of perfumed ointment on his head was to be included in the Gospel witness everywhere.

A sacrificial gift is an effective witness. Hearing of it can lead others to think of the devotion that is due our Lord and of how highly the Christian faith is valued by the giver.

- *For personal material gain*

In the Acts of the Apostles, Luke, a physician, tells of the good reception given to deacon Philip's preaching of the *"good news"* in Samaria (8:4-13). Learning of this the apostles in Jerusalem agreed that Peter and John should go there to help establish the new believers.

A famous magician in Samaria named Simon had professed faith in Christ. As a magician, Simon was much impressed by the spiritual powers displayed when these visiting apostles began to lay hands on various people, praying for them.

Making what seemed to him to be a decent proposal, Simon offered Peter and John money in exchange for his request that they might *"give me also this power."*

Simon was severely rebuked for that selfish request and in fact Peter's response was a curse that *"your money perish with you, because you thought you could obtain the gift of God with money"* (see Ac 8:18-29).

Giving with hope of personal gain deserves severe rebuke. To young Timothy, Paul offered the following warning about those who would profit from piety: *"those who are depraved in mind and bereft of the truth, imagining that godliness is a means of gain"* (1 Tm 6:5).

- *With hope of achieving merit*

The first eleven chapters of Paul's letter to the Romans contains one of the most comprehensive portrayals of the mercies of God found in the New Testament. This segment ends with the exclamatory question: *"Who has given a gift to [God] to receive a gift in return?"* (11:35).

Even should Christians be regularly giving much more than a tithe of their net income, or were laboring tirelessly out of devotion to their divine master, they could not merit blessings from God. To believe that merit is earned by giving offerings, or by rendering service to God, is to misunderstand or ignore what God has done for us, especially in view of our Savior's incarnation and death.

Once at a conference in the Philippines a thoughtful layperson asked me, "Why is it considered evil for those people who believe that they deserve a reward for what they have done?"

Someone else chimed in with a response, venturing: "It would be as though God and I were on an equal footing. If I do something for God, then God has to do something for me. Then what Christ has done for me is nothing. Redeemed sinners are not on a bargaining level with God who sacrificed his Son for us."

When Paul raised this question of giving a gift to God in order to be repaid, he did not leave the question unanswered. He replied, *"For from him and through him and to him are all things"* (Rm 11:33-36).

Self-seeking giving shrinks the heart and soul of the giver.

- *To be relieved of pressure*

As noted, Paul in his comprehensive passage on giving (2 Co 8 and 9) stated that, *"Each of you must give as you have made up your mind, not reluctantly or under compulsion, for God loves a cheerful giver."* (9:7).

Paul had been discussing the magnanimity of the Macedonian Christians who, though extremely poor, gave liberally for the famine sufferers with a "wealth of generosity . . . begging us earnestly for the privilege of sharing in this ministry to the saints" (8:4).

No pressure whatever was placed on those Macedonian Christians to give. In spite of their very trying circumstances they gave abundantly; they even felt they had been shown a favor to have the opportunity to give.

Good Motives

- *To express gratitude*

Among the many roots of a tree is a taproot, the most vital of the roots for it reaches down from the center of the trunk of the tree, goes the deepest and produces many little roots. This root contributes most to the stability, strength and productivity of the tree.

In the life of the Christian, gratitude is the spiritual taproot.

In his volume, *The Sense of the Presence of God,* John Baillie says,

> Gratitude not only is the dominant note in Christian piety. It is equally the dominant note of Christian action (p. 236).

The great giving of God exceeds what human beings can comprehend. We would do well to often meditate on the goodness of God so that a portion of the immensity of God's goodness might enter our awareness and thus help us increase our appreciation, as it did many psalmists of old.

Thus we read in Psalm 103:1, *"Bless the Lord, O my soul; and all that is within me, bless his holy name! Bless the Lord, O my soul and forget not all his benefits . . ."*

When Jesus healed the ten lepers and only one returned to thank him, he asked, *"Were there not ten restored, where are the nine?"* (Lk 17:17).

It seems Christ asked this question very sadly. May it not have been because he knew that by not being deeply grateful, they were missing blessings that could only be experienced by an appreciative heart? Gratitude expands the mind and heart to provide room for more joy.

Surely one reason so much light, power and joy poured out of the life of the apostle Paul was because he overflowed with thankfulness. Even though he experienced imprisonments, beatings, stonings, shipwrecks and myriad hardships, he could write: *"Thanks be to God, who in Christ always leads us in triumph"* (2 Co 2:14).

On this same note, Paul ended his longest appeal for giving with an exclamation of gratitude: *"Thanks be to God for his inexpressible gift!"* (2 Co 9:15). He began that appeal reminding his friends in Corinth of God's grace which in turn had inspired Macedonian believers to give "beyond their means." Then Paul concludes, *"You know the grace of our Lord Jesus Christ, that though he was* rich, yet for your sakes he became poor, so that by his poverty you might be rich" (2 Co 8:9).

The psalmist who asked, *"What shall I render to the Lord for all his bounty to me?"* answered the question, *"I will offer to thee the sacrifice of thanksgiving"* (Ps 116:12, 17).

- *To express love*

At the end of an evening worship service in Mexico where I had spoken, the local pastor who had interpreted for me said, "I think there are those who would like to ask questions."

The first questioner was the choir director: "Do you think a person can be a Christian without giving?"

I responded with another question: "Do you think a person can be a Christian without loving?"

The immediate reply was: "Certainly not! The Great Commandment is 'You must love God with all your heart.'"

I then continued, "Could a husband or a wife love each other without giving to the other?"

The response was immediate: "Impossible!"

The choir director then agreed that the question had been answered.

In the passage of 2 Corinthians referred above, Paul counsels: *"So, give proof . . . of your love."*

Jesus made the same challenge: *"Where your treasure is, there will your heart be also"* (Mt 6:21).

FIRST FRUITS

To love God with the whole heart is to do so cheerfully, serving God joyfully with our time, our abilities and the fruits of our labors — which are obtained with God-given time, God-furnished abilities and God-provided material resources.

High in the mountains of an island in the Philippines 14 families regularly gathered for Sunday school in one of their small homes. They longed for a little church where they might worship when their pastor who ministered to 17 far-flung congregations was able to be with them. After many years, out of their meager incomes from the sale of their crops — mostly corn and sweet potatoes grown on the steep slopes — they had gathered almost enough funds to start building a small chapel.

One Sunday Rosalita, a teenager, went home with her parents after worship and surprised them by confidently saying, "We're going to build our church!"

"Where will we get the money that we still need?" said the father.

"I'm going to give it," said Rosalita.

"Are you crazy?" retorted her father, "You haven't a penny. It will take many hundreds of bushel baskets of corn and potatoes still before we can start."

"God has shown me how," protested Rosalita.

God had shown her how. Rosalita got permission from her parents to leave their cool mountain home and go down to the steamy provincial capital to work. With the help of an uncle she secured a position in the home of a large family where in the heat of the tropics she worked hard many hours daily. When her wages added up to what was needed to start building the church, Rosalita went home with her earnings and gave it all for the new church.

Shortly after this we were concluding a stewardship study program at a seaside church in the provincial capital which both Rosalita and her pastor attended. The pastor shared with me the story of Rosalita's dedication to building a chapel in her home village and invited me to go visit that community. The chapel still had no walls, but it had a roof and they were going to dedicate the building as is.

An evening ride on a bus and a long hike on a shortcut mountain trail with the pastor, Rosalita and a lantern bearer got us to Rosalita's home by 3:00 A.M. After a bit of rest and a breakfast of roasted corn and boiled sweet potatoes, in the dawning light we joined the 14 families for the first service of worship to be held in that chapel. Somehow between our predawn arrival and this early morning meeting Rosalita had gotten the word of the gathering to all their surrounding neighbors.

As we raised our voices in praise to the God who loves us and blesses us bountifully each passing day, one person of that little congregation was not able to join in the singing. Rosalita's tears of joy streamed down her face so she could only sing with her heart. It was no surprise later to learn that Rosalita had dedicated her life to full-time church work and had entered a Bible school to prepare for a life of loving service to God.

The measure of giving sacrificially is the measure of loving. *"God so loved the world that he gave . . ."* The

Christian is one in whom God, who is love, dwells. The apostle Peter ended his second letter urging his readers to *"grow in the grace and knowledge of our Lord and Savior Jesus Christ"* (3:18). The grace of Jesus is Christ's out-going love.

With a few short lines John Oxenham defines love:

> Love ever gives
> Forgives, outlives-
> And ever stands
> With open hands
> And while it lives
> It gives.
> For this is love's prerogative
> To give and give, and give.

The true Christian steward gives because of being love-bound more than being duty-bound.

- *The desire to honor God*

The presentation of offerings has been a part of the worship of God according to the biblical record ever since Abel did it with *"the firstlings of his flock"* (Gn 4:4). And Proverbs clearly prioritized how we are to give: *"Honor the Lord with your substance and with the first fruits of all your produce"* (3:9).

Early in the New Testament account there is a beautiful example of offerings that truly render honor — gifts of gold, frankincense and myrrh (Mt 2:11) — for these are costly, fragrant and pure offerings. Happily there have been many such examples and still are. Our Lord, the Most High, is worthy of the best in worship and service.

In the last book of the Bible there is a description of what the worship of God will be like when worship is not marred by the weaknesses of humanity's earthly existence:

> *And when the living creatures give glory and honor and thanks to him who is seated on the throne, who lives for ever and ever, the 24 elders bow down before him who is seated on the throne, saying, "Worthy art thou, our Lord and God, to receive glory and honor and power, for thou didst create all things and by thy will they existed and were created* (Rv 4:9-11).

- *The desire to share in Christ's continuing mission*

A large part of Jesus' teaching of The Twelve, as recorded in the four Gospels, was intended for their guidance in instructing new believers as they would carry out The Great Commission: *"Go . . . make disciples of all nations . . . teaching them to observe all that I have commanded you"* (Mt 28:19-20). Christ explained that all *"must give up all right to themselves, to take up their cross and follow me"* (Mk 8:34). Thus one of his last commands to them was: *"As the Father has sent me, even so I send you"* (Jn 20:21).

Paul wrote to the Philippian Christians: *"It has been granted you that for the sake of Christ you should not only believe in him but also suffer for him"* (Ph 1:29). This they had already seen: James, the brother of John, had been cut down by Herod's sword and Stephen had been stoned by a Jerusalem mob. Out of gratitude and love, these and many other faithful stewards of the Gospel of the Early Church sacrificed their lives in continuing the mission for which their master had given all.

Together with this broad vision of the mission of stewards of the Gospel, Paul did not overlook the important concerns of new congregations. To the churches of Galatia he wrote : *"Those who are taught the word must share in all good things with their teacher"* (6:6). To the church in Corinth he wrote: *"If we have sown spiritual good things among you, is it too much if we reap your material benefits?"* (1 Co 9:11).

Paul listed nine simple illustrations to help them sense the reasonableness of Jesus' word about supporting Gospel messengers — those who devote their lives professionally in continuing Christ's mission in the world:

- The soldier doesn't bear his own expenses.
- The laborer in the vineyard gets fruit from it.
- The shepherd receives milk from the flock.
- The ox is permitted to eat from the grain that is being tread.
- The plowman plows with hope.
- The sower has a right to reap.
- The thresher expects to share in the harvest.

- The Levite in the temple received part of the sacrificial offerings.
- The priest shared in the sacrificial offerings.

(See 1 Co 9:7-14)

Paul's bottom line was: *"In the same way, the Lord commands that those who proclaim the gospel shall get their living by the Gospel"* (v. 14).

If we sincerely pray for God's kingdom to come and God's will to be done by having more laborers in the Gospel harvest field, then we will eagerly do what we can, supporting programs for preparation of laborers and for sustaining the workers as they strive locally and in global fields. Those needed laborers are doctors, nurses, evangelists, pastors, teachers, agriculturists and other persons who out of holy compassion help spread the Gospel and show God's compassion for the needy.

Part 4

Results for the Faithful

and Wise Steward

Introduction

We do not say "rewards for the faithful and wise stewards." If what is done is done out of love, the doer has no thought of reward. If the doing is done out of love and gratitude and out of a desire to honor another, how can it possibly be done with hope of being rewarded?

Paul's question that we have noted, *"Who has given a gift to [God] to receive a gift in return?"* (Rm 11:35) is actually a quote from the book of Job which ends with *"Whatever is under the whole heaven is mine"* (41:11).

Thus any rewards received should be unexpected. In Jesus' parable of the workers who arrived to begin their work at different times of the day, it was those who expressed concern about their rewards who were humiliated by the master (see Mt 20:9-16).

In the Final Judgment parable of Matthew 25 the persons rewarded were surprised that they were. This is reiterated in a book about the life of the apostle Paul written by James S. Stewart:

> . . . while for the idea that a man may put God in his debt by his obedience, the fact is that even if he were to wear his fingers to the bone in God's service, even if he were to burn

out his brain and beggar his soul in utter devotion, he still would not so much as have begun to establish a claim upon God. No man can ever have God in his debt. God has every man immeasurably in his" *A Man In Christ,* (pp. 86-87).

Thus we will look at five results for the faithful and wise steward of God who:

- Experiences Fullness of Life
- Is Given More Opportunity to Serve
- Encounters Special Joy
- Will Be Honored by the Heavenly Father
- Has an Intimate Relationship with God

14

Experience Fullness of Life

To persons in Colossae who had become *"alive together with Christ,"* Paul wrote *"You have come to the fullness of life in him who is the head of all rule and authority"* (2:10). To Timothy Paul explained that those who would be *"rich in good deeds, liberal and generous"* would be able to *"lay hold on the life which is life indeed"* (1 Tm 6:18-19).

Paul promises the same fullness of life when he writes to the Christians in Corinth about giving for relief of famine sufferers: *"The one who sows sparingly will also reap sparingly, and the one who sows bountifully will also reap bountifully"* (2 Co 9:6).

The Greek Church Father, John Chrysostom, some three centuries after Paul, said that giving can be spoken of as sowing because the giver gets more than was given.

When through the Christian steward there flows the compassion of God — expressed in generous and sympathetic giving of thought, of strength and of substance — in serving the needy, the Christian steward's life is inevitably greatly enriched.

To accept that which the divine master authorizes and guides one into, is to be assured of the most wholesome, abundant life.

15

Opportunity for More Service

We have noted that in one of his stewardship parables Jesus declared that a master said to his good servant, *"Well done, good and faithful servant; you have been faithful over a little, I will set you over much"* (Mt. 25:21).

Because the servant had been obedient and industrious in the use of those talents that had been entrusted to him, he was given opportunity to render more service for his master. Thus he enjoyed more confidence from his master and more intimate association with him.

In the Acts of the Apostles there is reference to a farmer by the name of Barnabas. We know of him first because he not only gave of his income to help those in need, he sold a field in order to have more money to share (4:36-37).

This first service opened up new opportunities for Barnabas. It was he who later helped the apostles become acquainted with and trust Saul — their recent persecutor who had been arresting Christians in order that they be put to death. Later it was Barnabas who was sent to Antioch to establish the new believers there. It was he who was chosen by the Holy Spirit to be Paul's first companion and guide in his great missionary journeys (see Ac 9:27, 11:22-26, 12:25, 13:2).

Barnabas was faithful with a material trust that may have seemed to him to have been a little matter, but that loyalty to Christ led to a ministry with Paul that has had immeasurable effect throughout the world for almost 20 centuries.

In the eleventh, twelfth and thirteenth chapters of the Acts of the Apostles where Luke describes the labors Paul and Barnabas engaged in together, he refers to them three times as *"Barnabas and Saul"* — naming Barnabas first. Does that not imply that Barnabas was the leader of the team for some time?

Near the time of his crucifixion Jesus said to his disciples: *"You did not choose me, but I chose you and appointed you that you should go and bear fruit and that your fruit should abide"* (Jn 15:16).

Faithful stewards can anticipate that the effects of their stewardship will continue through successive generations, as have the effects of the good stewardship of Barnabas.

16

Encounters Special Joy

In Jesus' parable of the Talents one servant was entrusted with five valuable talents, one with three and a third with one talent. The first two servants were industriously faithful in using the talents entrusted to them so when they reported their earnings, they heard, *"Well done, good and faithful servant; enter into the joy of your master"* (Mt 25:21).

The purest joy of the Christian is not experienced from material acquisition but from a right relationship with the divine master, which makes possible this magnificent sharing of Christ's joy.

Our Lord assured his disciples that they could experience complete joy, explaining that, *"If you keep my commandments, you will abide in my love, just as I have kept my Father's commandments and abide in his love. These things I have spoken to you, that my joy may be in you and that your joy may be full"* (Jn 15:10,11).

To worship God sincerely and obey God gladly is to experience that divine joy which Peter said was *"unutterable and exalted joy"* (1 P 1:8). The angel who announced the birth of Jesus to the shepherds said that he was bringing *"good news of great joy"* for all people. This joy would be for all who acknowledge the coming One, not only as Savior, but also as *"Christ and Lord."*

Once a Filipino doctor who was treasurer of his church told me of a poor employee at his hospital who sometimes was scheduled to work on Sunday and so then would give her weekly offering to him since she knew that she would not be able to be at the worship service. One week she came to him with more than the usual amount. He asked her why and she explained that the pastor had asked for a special offering to help the typhoon victims on another island.

"That's too much for you to give," the kind doctor said to her. Taking from his pocket an amount equal to the woman's extra, he said he would give that extra for her. She started to cry, the doctor said, so I said, 'I'm trying to help you!' " She shook her head and finally was able to say, 'You're taking from me the greatest joy I have in my life!' "

Obviously this dedicated woman was like the grace-filled new believers of Macedonia who in the *"abundance of joy and their extreme poverty"* begged the apostle Paul *"for the favor of taking part in relief of the saints"* (see 2 Co 8:1-4).

17

Will be Honored by God

It is easy to understand why we should honor the Almighty, Eternal God. It is not so easy to believe that the Eternal, Almighty God will in turn honor us mortals. But Jesus said, *"If anyone serves me, he must follow me; and where I am, there shall my servant be also; if any man serves me, the Father will honor him"* (Jn 12:26).

Jesus implied the same in that strange Parable of the Watchful Slaves when he said, *"Blessed are those slaves whom the master finds alert when he comes; truly I tell you, he will fasten his belt and have them sit to eat, and he will come and serve them"* (Lk 12:37).

In fact Christ demonstrated this highly improbable act in the Upper Room there in Jerusalem the night before he was crucified (see Jn 13:1-11). Here we see the Creator of All kneeling at the soiled feet of his sinful followers to wash their feet. Incredibly, this even included the dusty feet of the one he knew who would shortly betray him to death.

Should some day we find that the Lord of All is in some way honoring us, his unworthy servants, we will surely, in keeping with Peter's protestation, cry out, "How can You do this to us?"

Jesus would most likely explain, "You would understand, if you knew the meaning of Bethlehem and Calvary more truly."

18

Has an Intimate Relationship with God

Is there still more? For the faithful and wise steward there is. When a disciple, Judas (not the Iscariot), asked Jesus, *"Lord, how is it that you will manifest yourself to us and not to the world?"* Jesus made it clear that faithful stewards were to know him very intimately, for he answered Judas:

> *Those who love me will keep my word, and my Father will love them, and we will come to them and make our home with them* (Jn 14:23).

Most of all it is in the home where love is deeply felt and intimately shared. Yet we are told that there is a bond forged between the faithful Christian steward and the master which is stronger than that between members of the human family.

This is born out in Scriptures, for the author of the Gospel of Luke tells of the time when Jesus' mother and his brothers could not get to him to speak to him because so many were crowding about him to hear him. Word was passed to Jesus of their desire to speak to him. To all he announced the wonderful promise:

> *My mother and my brothers are those who hear the word of God and do it* (Lk 8:21).

Epilogue

The history of the church down through the ages has demonstrated that our God lovingly embraces the whole world with unspeakable sacrifices. Thus the call to Christian stewardship is merely to continue what God already is doing through sacrificial living, worshiping and serving the needy world for God's glory.

> *For it has been granted you that for the sake of Christ you should not only believe in his name but also suffer for his sake* (Ph 1:29).

Faithful and informed stewards of the divine master think much of what God has done for them and continues to do for them. They think of the wounds he has healed, of the burdens he has lifted, the countless other blessings he has freely given and the promises of more to come. Thus Christian stewards love and adore their Lord and with joy serve Christ and sacrifice for Christ with heart, soul, mind and strength.

As the apostle Paul called the believers in Rome to be good stewards of God, we are called to *"present your bodies as living sacrifice, holy, acceptable to God which is your reasonable service."* (Rm 12:1)

FIRST FRUITS

We give Thee but Thine own:
What-e'er that gift may be:
All that we have is Thine alone,
A trust, O Lord, from Thee,

May we Thy bounties thus
As stewards true receive,
And gladly, as Thou blessest us,
To Thee our first fruits give.

—Bishop W. Walsham How

References Cited

John Baillie, *The Sense of the Presence of God,* New York: Scribner, 1962.

Emil Brunner, *The Christian Doctrine of Creation and Redemption*, Philadelphia: Westminster Press, 1946.

George A. Buttrick, *Faith and Education*, New York: Abingdon-Cokesbury Press, 1952.

Sherwood Eddy, *Eighty Adventurous Years: An Autobiography,* New York: Harpers, 1954.

James S. Stewart, *A Man In Christ,* London: Hodder & Stoughton, 1935.

Bishop William Temple, *Nature, Man and God*, London: Macmillan & Co., 1935.

Paul Lindholm, D.D., distinguished authority on Christian stewardship, is widely recognized for the "imagination, thoroughness and spiritual content" he brings to this issue. He and his wife Clara served as missionaries for 39 years in China, India and the Philippines. He has traveled the world giving seminars on stewardship education and involved in this subject. Currently the Lindholms are living in active retirement in Duarte, California.

Additional copies of this book may be obtained
from your local bookstore,
or by sending $13.95 per paperback copy, postpaid,
or $20.95 per library hardcover copy, postpaid,
to:

**Hope Publishing House
P.O. Box 60008
Pasadena, CA 91116**

CA residents kindly add 8% sales tax

FAX orders to: (818) 792-2121

Telephone VISA/MC orders to: (800) 326-2671